Making Your Own Incense

Tina Sams & Maryanne Schwartz

CONTENTS

The Essence of Incense

Incense evokes a sense of luxury, of being in an exotic place where spices and aromas lift our spirits. The popularity of aromatherapy has led to a growing interest in incense as a means to make our homes more welcoming, more inviting, more pleasant. Unfortunately, commercial incenses rarely contain true essential oils or resins. Making your own incense can ensure that you're burning what you want!

Incense has been burned for thousands of years. Remember the wonderful tale of the Three Wise Men bearing gifts of frankincense and myrrh to baby Jesus? These gifts of the Magi were incenses highly valued for their fragrances. To this day, frankincense and myrrh are the most well-known resins used as incense.

In many Roman Catholic and Eastern Orthodox churches, incense mixtures containing frankincense and myrrh are still burned during sacred rituals.

What's a Resin?

A resin is derived from the sap of plants. Once processed, it resembles tiny tan or brown pebbles. Both frankincense and myrrh are resins; frankincense comes from the *Boswellia carteri* plant, native to Ethiopia, and myrrh comes from the *Commiphora myrrha* plant, which grows throughout northern Africa.

Many people associate incense with religious rituals or spirituality, and indeed, many religions use fragrant smoke in their rites and ceremonies. The smoke is said to sanctify, and many believe that it carries messages to the heavens. In addition, the smoke from smoldering incense is said to clear the air for "higher thinking," as might be needed for meditation.

During the Renaissance scents were used freely to disguise body odors because bathing was deemed unsafe. Hygiene at the time was at an all-time low as a previously rural population shifted to villages and cities that had poor or no sanitation provisions; many people used incense in their homes because they thought it would protect them against the plague and other diseases. As it turns out, this theory may have had some validity—many of the incense herbs, including thyme and lemongrass, have since been proved to contain healing and antiseptic properties.

In our homes, incense has been burned as a way both to mask unpleasant smells and to create an inviting, warm atmosphere. Long before the invention of aerosol cans, incense was a natural air freshener. Our grandmother often burned balsam incense cones in a little "smoking man" burner or a "Swiss chalet" that released smoke through its chimney. As children, they fascinated us!

The Science Behind the Scent

Throughout this booklet, we will refer to the aromatherapy bene-fits of the plants and other materials used to make incense. Every plant material contains essential oils—some incense recipes call for the essential oil itself, which is expressed from the plant through a special process and can be purchased at most herb shops. When we burn incense, molecules of these essential oils are released into the air. There they find their way through our olfactory system and through the pores in our skin to our brain, where they effect chemi-cal interactions that can change our mood, evoke memories of times past, and more. These aromas can help us to relax or to wake up; they can raise our spirits or even put us into romantic moods! In fact, some essential oils have been proven to hold many healing proper-ties; thyme, for example, was used to disinfect hospitals and sick-rooms until the discovery of modern antibiotics.

Crafting Our First Incense

We discovered the joys of burning real incense several years ago when we were "The Herb Ladies" at a Renaissance Faire in Pennsylvania. It seemed fitting to use the scent of burning resins to lure throngs of visitors to our little herb shop. The resins and herbs we burned seemed to help lift our spirits—as well as the spirits of those entering the shop.

We sold resins by the ounce and kept a bag filled with the bits left over after dividing up pounds. Inside our bag were chunks of

Types of Incense

As you may have guessed, there are different types of incense. Here's the lineup:

- Smudge
- Loose noncombustibles
- Loose combustibles
- Combustible cones and sticks

The "combustible" and "noncombustible" labels simply tell you whether or not the incense mixture contains a combustible ingredient—that is, whether the incense will burn on its own if it is lit with a match or whether you need to combine it with something else that burns readily, like charcoal, in order for it to ignite.

frankincense and myrrh along with dragon's blood, benzoin, copal, sandalwood and other woods, and herbs and spices. We burned a charcoal block and sprinkled our "blend" on it from time to time. People often asked us what we were burning. We couldn't answer them honestly because it was always just a wonderful mishmash of whatever had landed in our bag at that time.

Burning a combination like this is easy outdoors, where the aromas dissipate into wonderful clouds. Inside, however, it's a different matter. When we attempted to burn our blend inside a closed house, the billows of fragrance no longer dissipated; instead, they filled the rooms with heavy, resinous smoke. We were disappointed. How could we reproduce that scent inside without the smoke overcoming us?

We searched for incense sticks or cones that smelled the same as the resins we had burned. Occasionally we found commercial incense made with the actual resins, but they were quite expensive. Other times, we found products labeled FRANKINCENSE or DRAGON'S BLOOD, but it was obvious that they had been created by people who had never smelled the real thing. To us, they smelled suspiciously like cinnamon or synthetics.

Finally, we found some vague directions and recipes for handmade incense. It still took us quite a while to assemble the ingredients. It was difficult to find saltpeter, the combustible ingredient that keeps incense smoldering, and the gums used as "glue" to hold the incense together weren't the kind of thing you can pick up in your local grocery store. Eventually we found what we needed and started playing around with ingredients and recipes. The instructions never seemed to be clear enough, but, through trial and error, we finally formulated some recipes that worked.

Once we became more confident in our ability to create true incense, we started giving classes at our shop. Teaching people to make their own incense has become one of our goals.

Choosing the Right Ingredients

Here's a basic checklist of all the ingredients used to make incense. Different types of incense call for different types of ingredients, of course, so you may not need all of these items:

- Fragrant woods
- Resins
- Gums
- Herbs and spices
- Oils
- Pyrotechnics

Researching the ingredients for incense is enough to give one a feeling of wanderlust! The names, descriptions, and locations of the various ingredients sweep us away to other times and places. Often, we picture an exotic bazaar where the stalls are loaded with wonderfully fragrant woods, herbs, spices, and oils. In our minds, we picture vivid colors—reds and yellows—and bright sunlight.

Fragrant Woods

Woods suitable for incense come in many choices and fragrances. Their moisture content and density affect how quickly and evenly the incense burns. Wood is best incorporated into incense when it is powdered. We like hanging around our woodworking relatives and grabbing the resulting sawdust. If you don't have access to the sawdust of fragrant woods, you can buy powdered woods at many herb shops and places that sell incense.

> **Quick Tip**
>
> Store sawdust in clean, air-tight containers in a cool, dark location. Always label the containers so that you'll know what type of wood they contain.

Following are what we think are some of the best fragrant woods to use in incense.

Evergreen woods (pine, fir, spruce, arborvitae, cedar)
Evergreens are wonderful for making incense. In fact, because their wood is so resinous, it is often used alone as incense. Balsam incense, a very popular product in incense shops, is made solely from the wood of the evergreen balsalm fir.

Red cedar (*Juniperus virginiana*)
Red cedar sawdust is a pale red powder that makes a wonderful base for incense mixtures. It's used in many insect repellent combinations and would probably team well with other repellents for an outdoor, pre-picnic incense. The scent of red cedar is said to encourage a sense of balance and calm.

Sandalwood, red (*Pterocarpus santalinus*)
A few years ago, it was nearly impossible to obtain yellow sandalwood, the type of sandalwood most often used in incense, and red became a popular replacement. Also known as santal, red sandalwood is similar in fragrance to the yellow but lacks its full, earthy tones. It is still a good base, particularly if you want a less pronounced wood scent.

Sandalwood, yellow (*Santalum album*)
Yellow sandalwood, often called simply sandalwood, is one of the most commonly used woods in incense making. It has a rich, exotic fragrance that blends well with just about everything and is said to

encourage a sense of inner calm. The finest of all sandalwoods comes from the Mysore region of India. Sandalwood oil has been in great demand there for many years, which has caused concern about over-harvesting and the region's ecological balance. Currently, the only sandalwood oil and wood available for export are made from the waste chippings from religious carvings. As a result, Mysore sandalwood is in very short supply and its price is greatly inflated.

Wild cherry (*Prunus* spp.) and other fruit woods

The wood from wild cherry trees burns with an almond scent, which we first noticed when putting some small wild cherry trees through a mulcher. The fresher the wood powder, the higher the concentration of the plant's essential oils and the greater the scent. Other fruit woods are wonderful, too. People have coveted these woods for burning on the hearth for years; we just save the sawdust for incense.

Resins

Of all the ingredients used in incense, resins impart the heaviest scent. All resins are sticky because they are derived from plant sap. They can be purchased in hard rocks or in powdered form—although the powders tend to reform pretty quickly back into rocks. We put the rocks into plastic bags, pulverize them with a hammer, and then grind them to a powder in a coffee grinder earmarked for resins only. (Any implements you use for grinding resins will most likely be ruined for any other use.)

On the following pages, you'll find brief descriptions of our six favorite resins.

Tips for Grinding Resins

- Grind only the amount of resin that you need because any leftover powdered resin will reform into rocks that need to be ground again.
- Grinding citrus peels can help clean your grinder after you use it to grind resin.

Smokeless Resins

To get the smell of resins without the smoke, simmer them in water. Use about 1 tablespoon (15 ml) of resins per cup (240 ml) of water. We often simmer frankincense in water to lessen its powerful scent.

Caution: Don't use your favorite pan for simmering resins— this process leaves a gooey mess that is very difficult to clean.

Benzoin (*Styrax benzoin*)
Benzoin is often used as a preservative in cosmetics and soaps. Derived from a plant native to Sumatra, benzoin is white or tan in color and delivers a sweet vanilla scent. Because it is mild, benzoin can be paired with botanicals that are not powerful enough to come through over stronger resins. In aromatherapy, benzoin is recommended for its relaxing, calming properties.

Camphor (*Cinnamomum camphora*)
Native to China and Japan, the camphor plant offers an extremely aromatic resin. It clears the head but must be used in small quantities because it is so strong. In old songs and stories, "camphorated oil" is described as a chest rub good for treating congestion, cold sores, and fever blisters.

Copal (*Hymenaea courbaril*)
Derived from a Central American tree, copal is the frankincense of the Western World. The Mayans considered it food for the gods and used it during their worship ceremonies. There are many different grades and colors of copal. We use a pale yellow copal that is quite aromatic—it can best be described as a high, thin piney scent with a fuller woodsy background.

Dragon's blood (*Daemonerops draco*)
Draco, the species name of this Indonesian plant, means dragon, and dragon's blood is its sap. This resin is not easy to find, but it's worth the search. We receive it in 5-inch (13 cm) balls, stamped with gold seals, from Indonesia. It is a beautiful red, reminiscent of cinnabar, and incredibly sticky and has a deep, rich woodsy smell. When we burn it, people always want to know what it is. This resin is sometimes used in healing salves, as it is said to have antiseptic qualities.

Frankincense (*Boswellia carteri*)
This resin of biblical fame is derived from a plant native to Ethiopia and comes in pearl, tear, and powdered forms. (However, the powder reforms into chunks that must then be hammered into powder again.) Its scent is somewhat piney. Frankincense is often burned in sanctuaries prior to services—the first time we burned it, Maryanne said, "It smells just like the furniture polish they used in church!" Frankincense is said to be helpful for nervous conditions and tension.

Myrrh (*Commiphora myrrha*)
Another resin of biblical fame, myrrh can be found in many forms—small chunks, granulated, or powdered—and in varying shades of reddish brown. It comes from the sap of the myrrh tree, which is native to northern Africa. Rarely used alone, the deep, dark, almost haunting scent of myrrh is often combined with the sunnier frankincense. Myrrh is often used in toothpastes and mouthwashes because it helps heal gums and freshen breath.

Gums

We have used two types of gum to form the glue that holds together our stick and cone incense: gum arabic and gum tragacanth. To make the glue, we mix the gum with very warm water until it reaches a thick, sticky consistency. The gum transforms the incense from a mixture of powdered materials to a workable dough that can be easily formed into shapes.

Gum arabic (*Acacia* spp.)
Gum arabic, imported mainly from Sumatra, is relatively easy to find. Unfortunately, it is also less suitable for making incense (but then, it you weren't up for a challenge, you'd just buy the incense ready-made!). Two tablespoons (30 ml) mixed with 1 cup (240 ml) of very warm water makes a very sticky liquid, but the liquid often does not thicken as the package directions say it will. It works, however, even without thickening. You can also find premixed gum arabic in

art-supply stores under the name "spirit gum." This thick, gluey mixture is used for fastening on theatrical beards. It can also be used for making incense but must first be thinned with water.

Gum tragacanth (*Astragalus gummifer*)
Tragacanth, derived from a plant native to Europe, is the gum we prefer to use. A teaspoon (5 ml) of the powder in a cup (240 ml) of very warm water quickly thickens into glue. It is a bit more expensive than the gum arabic, but much less is needed. Tragacanth is used commercially as a thickener for foods such as gravy, ice cream, and pudding. Mix up only what you plan to use—for some reason the premixed stuff, even when kept just overnight, develops a disgusting stench.

Herbs and Spices

The list of botanicals you can add to incense blends is endless. We sometimes add pinches of sand from that unforgettable time spent on the beach, or a couple violet blossoms just because it is finally spring, or maybe just one petal from a very special rose. You get the idea.
Here are our favorite herbs and spices.

Allspice (*Pimenta dioica*)
Native to Jamaica and Mexico, allspice imparts a warm and spicy aroma, like a blend of cloves, juniper, cinnamon, and pepper. It is reputed to be stimulating and vitalizing and is used to treat depression, nervous exhaustion, and fatigue.

Basil (*Ocimum basilicum*)
The basil we use for incense is the same common herb used in pestos today. Basil is fragrant, herby, and lively—we love it combined with benzoin and cinnamon. Basil is said to be helpful for maintaining concentration and overcoming fatigue.

Bay (*Laurus nobilis*)
From the lands of Egypt and Turkey, this spicy herb has a stimulating and uplifting scent that soothes sinus headaches and revives those suffering from travel fatigue.

Cardamom (*Elettaria cardamomum*)
Cardamom smells wonderfully fresh and slightly lemony. We first discovered it when a friend added it to a kitchen incense—we were pleasantly surprised by the result. Cardamom is said to be helpful for soothing headaches—an interesting bit of trivia given that cardamom was traditionally an ingredient in love potions! It also helps to clear the mind and stimulate the appetite.

Cinnamon (*Cinnamomum cassia* or *C. zeylanicum*)
Believed to have originated in China, Indonesia, or Sri Lanka, cinnamon is a hot spice. For incense, we use the powdered bark. Cinnamon's essential oil acts as a stimulant, an antiseptic, and an antifungal—burn this one when fighting a viral infection.

Citrus peel
The peel from any of the citrus fruits—grapefruit, orange, lemon, lime, or kumquat, for example—is nice, but not as nice as one might expect. The essential oil is better because the peel begins to smell bitter after it has burned briefly. Most citruses have an uplifting, invigorating scent. Grapefruit, in particular, is exhilarating and energizing.

Cloves (*Syzygium aromaticum*)
Hailing originally from Madagascar or Indonesia, cloves are now cultivated worldwide and are easily available. They have a warm, spicy aroma that is said to act as a stimulant. Clove oil is often used as a topical antibacterial agent.

Coriander (*Coriandrum sativum*)
Coriander has a fresh, almost lemony aroma with an herby background—a wonderfully calming, uplifting scent for any kitchen.

Eucalyptus (*Eucalyptus globulus*)
Dried and ground eucalyptus leaves are very aromatic when burned. We do not suggest burning the preserved bluish green eucalyptus sold for use in crafts because its preservative is an allergen for many. Instead, search out the pale yellow-green eucalyptus, which can be purchased from herb shops, in bulk or loose form. We've found the herb to help clear the sinuses.

Evergreen needles
Evergreens come from a variety of plant families and have a wonderful scent—each species has its own subtle twist. White pine is the "piniest" in our part of the country but there are many other types to choose from. Evergreen needles are sticky and messy to prepare, but the result is so pleasant that it is worth the effort. Most evergreens are considered useful for clearing the head and refreshing the air.

Fennel seeds (*Foeniculum vulgare)*
Originally from India, fennel seeds smell like anise or licorice and are reputed to be helpful for menopausal problems.

Juniper berries (*Juniperus communis*)
Believed to have originated in Macedonia, these surprisingly fragrant berries deliver a heady blend of fruit and evergreen. We find that they smell like a mango tastes! Juniper oil is said to ease respiratory conditions.

Lavender (*Lavandula angustifolia*)
Lavender is one of the most popular aromatic herbs around. For incense, the freshly dried and ground herb work best. Lavender imparts a very fresh, clean scent and is used in aromatherapy to induce relaxation.

Lemongrass (*Cymbopogon citratus*)
Hailing from Guatemala and Peru, lemongrass has only a subtle scent after being dried.
Lemon grass has antiseptic properties and is
often burned as an insect repellent.

Lemon verbena (*Aloysia triphylla*)
Lemon verbena imparts a long-lasting, strong, pleasant lemon scent that is thought to be relaxing and
helpful for relieving stress.

Orrisroot (*Iris pallida*)
Orrisroot is the bulb of the iris. It acts as a preservative and is a popular ingredient in potpourri recipes. It has a faint violet scent. The
expensive oil is said to ease respiratory conditions, but we add the
powdered herb to incense mixtures for its fixative properties to keep scents from fading.

Patchouli (*Pogostemon cablin*)
A native of India, patchouli has a scent that we remember from the '60s. It originally came into popularity
long ago, when textiles imported from India
were packed in patchouli to protect them
from moths during the long trip. The scent
was considered quite exotic. There seems
to be no middle ground when it comes to
patchouli—it is a scent that is either loved
or despised.

Rosemary (*Rosmarinus officinalis*)
Rosemary has a fresh piney scent associated with
memory-enhancing properties and youth. Rosemary is currently
being studied for its potential in helping slow down memory loss in
Alzheimer's patients.

Sage (*Salvia* spp.)
With sage, a little goes a long way. We are fortunate to have received
some desert sage (*S. eremostachya*) from New Mexico, which we
think is the best. It's slightly camphorous, but definitely fragrant.
The herb is antibacterial and antifungal in nature.

Scented geraniums (*Pelargonium graveolens*)
Geranium is said to be useful for depression and menstrual problems. It has a full, flowery scent with a rose note.

Sweet grass (*Hierochloe odorata*)
Offering an inviting vanilla scent, this plant seems to have a calming, relaxing effect. It is best known as a sacred plant in Native American rituals.

Thyme (*Thymus* spp.)
Thyme has a definitive antiseptic scent. It acts as a general stimulant and is used in aromatherapy to treat fatigue and mental exhaustion.

We heartily recommend that you dry and use whatever herbs you can from your own garden. Adding ingredients that you've grown and harvested yourself enriches the entire experience.

Note: If you want to try out a new ingredient that you found while wandering field or forest, be sure that you can identify it first—even before gathering it—to make sure that it's neither a threatened nor a poisonous species. We always keep a good field guide nearby. If you aren't sure what it is, don't pick it and don't use it.

Words of Caution

Never use poisonous plants to make incense because the smoke can be just as dangerous as the plant itself. In addition, if you should notice any adverse reaction to an incense mixture, immediately stop burning it—crush out the smoldering ingredients and throw them outside. Make note of what that incense contained so that as you continue experimenting with different mixes, you can deduce which ingredient negatively affects you and stop using it.

The following are plants that you should never burn as incense:

- Boxwood
- Foxglove
- Jimsonweed
- Lily-of-the-valley
- Mistletoe
- Monkshood
- Narcissus or daffodil

- Members of the night-shade family (including belladonna, bittersweet, tomato, and eggplant)
- Oleander
- Poison ivy, sumac, or oak
- Wormwood

Essential Oils

Both synthetic fragrance oils and essential oils can easily be used to enhance incense, but only true essential oils will produce an aromethera-peutic effect. Before adding an oil to an incense mixture, be sure to burn a drop on charcoal. Most oils stay true when they burn, but some turn out to be not as pleasant as you might think. Fragrance oils, especially, which are made from synthetic sources (chemicals), may smell quite differently when burned than when in the bottle.

We sometimes add several drops of oil to our incense mixtures after the dough is mixed. How much depends on the size of the batch being made—at least one drop per spoonful of dry mix, more if a strong scent is desired. Don't overdo it—you can always add oil to the dried sticks and cones, but you can't take oil out once it's in there.

Oils can be used in place of a plant, to boost a plant's scent (lavender essential oil with ground lavender, for example), or to create a combination (such as musk oil with patchouli). However, many times we make incense with no oils added.

Our favorite essential oils are:

- Bergamot—acts as an antidepressant
- Jasmine or ylang-ylang—puts you in a romantic mood
- Lavender—when you want to relax
- Citrus oils, like grapefruit—to provide an energizing scent

Note: If you're interested in learning more about essential oils and how they work, you should consult some of the many fine books on aromatherapy that are available.

Pyrotechnics

The "pyrotechnics" of an incense mix is simply what makes the incense continue to burn after it has been lit and the flame then extinguished. We use saltpeter, or potassium nitrate, for this purpose. Charcoal blocks contain saltpeter; this is why, after they have been lit and the flame then blown out, they continue to smolder.

"Punk" Incense

You can sometimes find blank cones or sticks packaged and labeled as "punk." These wood bases contain saltpeter and are often sold in hardware stores in the spring and summer to burn as an insect repellent. Simply add a few drops of your favorite essential oil and burn. They're not bad, but handmade incenses are a completely different thing—as you will soon find out for yourself!

You will need saltpeter only when making combustible cones and sticks. Smudge sticks, which are composed of papery dried herbs, will burn on their own and do not need any additional form of pyrotechnics. Loose noncombustible incense is burned on charcoal blocks. Loose combustible incense contains powdered charcoal and does not need any additional saltpeter.

The recipes we've found state that saltpeter should comprise no more than 10 percent *by weight* of an incense mixture. When we follow this guideline, however, our incense does not always burn all the way down. We now think that the best rule is to add saltpeter so that it comprises slightly less than 10 percent *by volume*. This is less precise but easier to accomplish, especially since most people do not have access to a scale sensitive enough to measure down to $\frac{1}{100}$ of an ounce. We keep track of how many "parts" go into the mixing bowl and then add saltpeter in the amount of a little less than 10 percent by volume. For example, if there are 9 parts (or 9 teaspoons) in the bowl, then we use a pinch less than 1 part (or slightly less than 1 teaspoon); if there are 7 parts in the bowl, we use a pinch less than ¾ part. Measuring like this takes a bit of practice. A touch too much means the incense burns too fast. A lot too much means it will explode—so if you're making up your own recipes, be careful!

The amount of saltpeter called for in our recipes should be correct, although saltpeter can lose its "oomph" as it ages. If you have followed our instructions and your incense doesn't seem to burning properly, the saltpeter you're using may be old. Try using more in your next batch or finding a fresher batch of saltpeter.

Smudge and Smudge Sticks

The smudge type of incense uses herbs, loose or bundled. When lit, blown out, and then allowed to smolder, smudge incense fills the area with its fragrant smoke. For our purposes, smudge is a fun way to use the wonderfully fragrant herbs that we grow or that we find near our home. Lavender, monarda, scented geraniums, rosemary, thyme, and pine are pleasant choices. Resins can also be bound in with the herbs. They will melt and smolder along with the rest of the bundle.

Traditionally, smudge was burned by many native peoples to "clear the air" of negative energy or feelings or to bring good spirits. We use smudge ourselves to change the feeling of a place. For example, occasionally we will have a difficult customer or a difficult situation that will leave us with a bad feeling. We burn smudge and find that our spirits lift. Burning the smudge stick becomes a positive act that counteracts the negative feelings we had been having.

You can make your own smudge stick by bundling aromatic twigs together and tying them tightly with string (see page 18), or you can purchase ready-made smudge bundles at most herb shops. Commercial varieties of smudge sticks are tied with one continuous string, which burns in such a way that the plant material stays together as it burns.

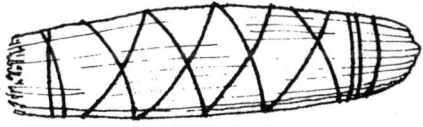

Smudge sticks are large or small bundles of herbs tied together with string.

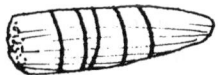

Christen Your New Home

You can make your new house quickly feel more like home if you smudge it with lavender in a homemade housewarming ritual. In addition to its delicate scent, lavender offers disinfectant and calming qualities.

Making a Smudge Stick

Step 1. Pick a bundle of herbs at least twice as thick as you would like the finished bundle to be. The best time to harvest is during early autumn, when plants have begun to dry naturally, yet still retain enough moisture to keep them from being brittle. Tie the base firmly with a string, leaving loose ends that are at least three times as long as the bundle.

Step 2. Crisscross the loose lengths of string up and around the length of the bundled herbs, forming a diamond pattern. Tie off at the top and trim the remaining string. Hang the bundle to dry in a well-ventilated location to prevent the herbs from molding. Check the tightness of the string each day and tighten it if it becomes loose. When it is dry, which will take 3 to 5 weeks, the smudge bundle will be relatively lightweight and the herbs will feel "crunchy" to touch.

Burning a Smudge Stick

Step 1. Light the smudge stick with a match, lighter, or the flame of a candle. It may take a few tries to get it burning well. Once the stick is burning, however, blow out the actual flame so that the stick is just smoldering and giving off a good amount of smoke.

Step 2. Lay the smudge stick in a bowl filled with sand or pebbles and allow it to burn, or "smudge" the area or person you are attempting to cleanse by carrying the smoldering bundle and fanning smoke toward or around that area or person.

Step 3. Depending on its size, a smudge stick will burn for anywhere from 15 minutes to 2 hours. Most users light them for only a short time, just long enough to accomplish the smudging they are intended for. When finished, extinguish the smudge stick by grinding it in a bowl filled with sand or pebbles.

Step 4. If there is enough of the smudge stick left to use again, wait for it to cool and then store it in an airtight container or zip-seal plastic bag.

Loose Noncombustible Incense

This type of incense is composed of loose herbs and resins that are burned on a charcoal block. These blocks are small compressed "pellets" of charcoal, not the type used for grilling food. Charcoal blocks are relatively inexpensive and come in rolls of five to ten or in boxes of forty. They can be purchased at most herb shops and any place that sells incense.

- **Rolls.** Each charcoal pellet in a roll is about 1 to 1½ inches (3–4 cm) in diameter and ½ inch (1 cm) thick. Each pellet has a slight depression in the middle where the botanical or resin is placed to smolder. This charcoal will burn for close to an hour.
- **Boxes.** The charcoal pellets sold in a box are more compressed and cleaner to handle. Each is about ½ inch (1 cm) square and about ¼ inch (5 mm) thick. They are flat—that is, they don't have a depression for holding the herb or resin— and will burn for only about 15 minutes or so.

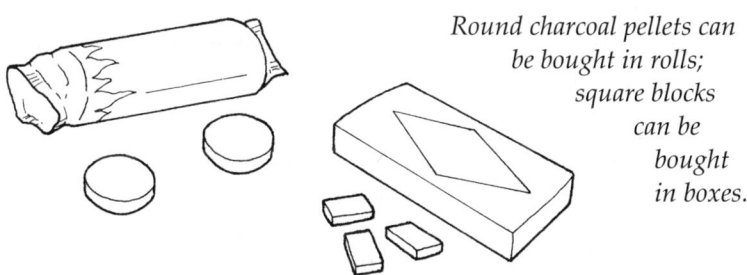

Round charcoal pellets can be bought in rolls; square blocks can be bought in boxes.

Charcoal pellets burn very hot and can damage surfaces and severely sear skin upon contact, so be careful when using them. The first time we tried burning incense on charcoal, Maryanne held the charcoal for too long after it was lit. When she felt the sparks of fire nipping at her fingers, she dropped it in an old ashtray, which cracked because the heat was so intense. (We've now learned to set the charcoal in a container filled with a material that will dissipate the heat, such as sea salt, sand, or gravel.)

Burning Loose Noncombustible Mix

Follow these steps (and cautions) when using loose noncombustible incense:

Step 1. Find the right location. This method is extremely smoky, so you may want to be outdoors or by an open window.

Step 2. Use a heatproof surface. Before lighting the charcoal, have a suitable container for it, such as a heatproof ceramic bowl or ashtray. Partially fill the container with sand, pebbles, or sea salt to dissipate the heat.

Step 3. Light the charcoal. Hold the charcoal securely, ideally with tongs, and light it by holding a lit match or lighter underneath it. As soon as you see sparks, put the charcoal down on the sand. When the sparkles spread over the block, it is ready.

Step 4. Place the loose mixture on the charcoal. Place pinches of the incense on the block. The herbs and resins will begin to smolder and the smoke will waft through the air, scenting the area.

Step 5. Extinguish the charcoal. The best way to extinguish the charcoal is to let it burn through. If you don't have time for that, however, simply crush the charcoal and dump the contents of the container outside or into a bowl of water.

To scent a large area, try burning essential or fragrance oils on charcoal. Citronella oil can be burned on a charcoal pellet at a picnic to very effectively clear the area of pesky insects. You can even burn the citronella right on the charcoal briquettes in a grill—just be sure that you're all done cooking food on the grill; otherwise, you'll be dining on citronella-flavored burgers.

Caution

Do not douse a lit piece of charcoal with water while it is burning in a container. The cold water hitting the hot container could cause the container to explode. Instead, crush out the burning charcoal and dump it in a container filled with water.

Loose Combustible Incense

Loose combustible incense consists of loose herbs, resins, and woods mixed with ground charcoal. Traditionally, it is shaped into a small pile, compressed with the fingers, and lit. The more tightly compressed the pile is, the better it will burn. This is a somewhat less smoky method of burning resins. We've rarely seen this type of incense for sale, so if you're interested in using it, your best bet is to make it yourself.

Making a Loose Combustible Mix

Loose combustible incense is quite easy to make. Simply mix together 3 parts of herbs, resins, gums, or fragrant woods with 1 part of powdered charcoal pellets. To powder the charcoal pellets, place them in a thick plastic bag and crush them with a hammer.

Combustible Cones and Sticks

Cones and sticks are what most people generally think of as incense. These solid forms, when lit, will smolder after the flame has been extinguished, giving off a scent. The handmade version of this incense is the most complicated to make, yet somehow the most satisfying.

We find that gum tragacanth is easier to use for our combustible incense recipes. However, you can use gum arabic if you prefer—see page 9 for mixing directions.

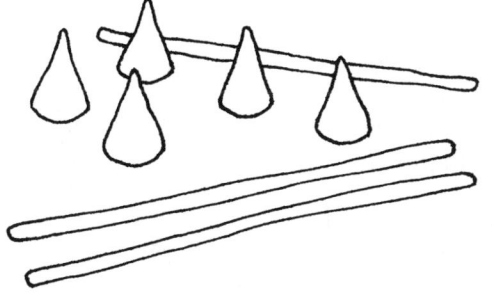

Combustible cones and sticks are what most people think of as incense.

Making Your Own Sticks and Cones

Step 1. Combine gum tragacanth with very warm water, using 1 cup (240 ml) of water for every teaspoon (5 ml) of gum tragacanth. Mix thoroughly. Set aside.

Step 2. Lay out a square of waxed paper on a level work surface.

Step 3. Choose your recipe and gather the ingredients. All ingredients should be finely ground before you get started.

Step 4. Using a large bowl and a fork or spoon, mix all the dry ingredients thoroughly.

> ### Quick Tip
> Place the waxed paper on top of a sheet of cardboard. This will protect your work surface and allow you to move the incense so it can be dried elsewhere.

Step 5. Add the glue, which by now should have become quite thick, in increments, adding just enough so that the mixture has the consistency of a child's play dough. (If you use too much glue, it's not the end of the world—the incense will simply take longer to dry and the cones might droop.)

Step 6. Add the fragrance or essential oils, if you're using them, and mix them in thoroughly with the dough.

Step 7. Shape the dough into cones, "snakes," sheets, or whatever shapes you desire.

> **To make a cone,** take a pinch, perhaps ½ to ¾ teaspoon (3–4 ml), and press it against one thumb to form the flat bottom while using the thumb and first two fingers of your other hand to create the cone shape. The first few tries (or batches) will look more like pyramids, but don't worry— it'll get easier with practice.
>
> *To make a cone, roll a pinch of dough between your thumb and first two fingers.*

To make a sheet, simply roll out the whole batch on waxed paper to about ¼ inch (0.6 cm) thickness. Trim the edges to make a square or rectangle. Score the sheet of incense so that there are postage stamp–size lozenges. These dry quickly and burn very well.

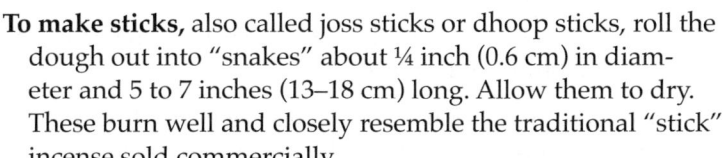

A scored sheet will yield "tabs" of incense that dry quickly.

To make sticks, also called joss sticks or dhoop sticks, roll the dough out into "snakes" about ¼ inch (0.6 cm) in diameter and 5 to 7 inches (13–18 cm) long. Allow them to dry. These burn well and closely resemble the traditional "stick" incense sold commercially.

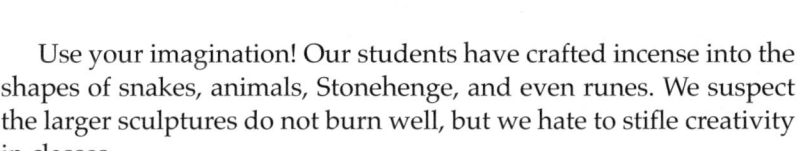

To make incense sticks, roll out the dough in long, think "snakes."

Use your imagination! Our students have crafted incense into the shapes of snakes, animals, Stonehenge, and even runes. We suspect the larger sculptures do not burn well, but we hate to stifle creativity in classes.

Step 8. Place the shaped incense pieces carefully on the sheet of waxed paper. Allow to dry for a day in a warm, dry location.

Step 9. After 24 hours, move the incense pieces around to help them dry: Tip over the cones, flip over sheets, or roll the snake. Continue turning daily until dry, about 3 or 4 days.

Step 10. After the incense pieces are thoroughly dry, they're ready to be burned. Until you do so, store the finished incense in airtight containers or zip-seal plastic bags.

Incense Recipes

Following is a collection of some of our favorite recipes. It should be noted that resins are interchangeable and that herbs and spices can be added or deleted, based on your preference. Woods can even be used alone if desired. You should, of course, expect some setbacks along the way, but that's part of the fun of learning your way around incense.

Now let's get started!

Loose Incense Mixtures

These simple mixtures of resins, woods, herbs, and oils are easy to mix and use. They can be sprinkled on smoldering charcoal or combined with powdered charcoal (see the box at right) and then lit.

PASSION

This mixture is deep red in color and has a rich earthy scent.

- 2 teaspoons (10 ml) dragon's blood
- 2 teaspoons (10 ml) dried patchouli
- 2 teaspoons (10 ml) powdered red sandalwood
- 1 teaspoon (5 ml) powdered orrisroot
- 14 drops musk or patchouli oil

FOREST FANTASY

One sniff and you will be transported to a pine forest. This is nice at Christmastime and could be simmered as well (see the box on page 8).

- 1 teaspoon (5 ml) frankincense
- 1 teaspoon (5 ml) powdered juniper wood
- 1 teaspoon (5 ml) powdered pine wood

SUNNY DAY

Housecleaning time is a favorite time for us to burn incense. This one seems to throw open the windows and let the sunshine in.

- 1 tablespoon (15 ml) frankincense
- 1 teaspoon (5 ml) ground cinnamon bark
- ½ teaspoon (3 ml) dried rosemary
- 12 drops orange oil

Making Loose Combustible Incense

To make loose combustible incense, simply add powdered charcoal to these incense mixtures, using 1 teaspoon (5 ml) of powdered charcoal for every 3 teaspoons (15 ml) of incense.

WARM WOODS

This blend is piney and spicy at the same time!

1   tablespoon (15 ml) pine needles
1   teaspoon (5 ml) cardamom seed
1   teaspoon (5 ml) grains of paradise (available in most
      herb shops)

RELAXING

The mellow scent of this blend helps with stress.

1   teaspoon (5 ml) sandalwood
1   teaspoon (5 ml) lavender

Combustible Solid Incense

Please note that although we call for gum tragacanth in these recipes, you can also use gum arabic. See page 9 for mixing instructions.

CEDAR, SAGE, AND COPAL

This recipe combines the ingredients commonly used in a popular smudge stick for a very cleansing blend.

½   teaspoon (3 ml) gum tragacanth
½   cup (120 ml) very warm water
2   tablespoons (30 ml) powdered cedar
2   teaspoons (10 ml) copal
2   teaspoons (10 ml) dried sage
1   teaspoon (5 ml) powdered orrisroot
1   teaspoon (5 ml) saltpeter

Combine the ingredients as directed on pages 22–23. Shape incense as desired and allow to dry.

DRAGON'S BLOOD

This is a great recipe for pure resin fragrance. Any resin can be substituted for the dragon's blood.

½ teaspoon (3 ml) gum tragacanth
½ cup (120 ml) very warm water
3 tablespoons (45 ml) wood of your choice
1 tablespoon (15 ml) dragon's blood
1 teaspoon (5 ml) powdered orrisroot
1–1¼ teaspoons (5–6 ml) saltpeter

Combine the ingredients as directed on pages 22–23. Shape incense as desired and allow to dry.

SANDALWOOD

This recipe can be used for any of the woods—just substitute the wood of your choice for sandalwood. Benzoin adds a mild vanilla fragrance.

½ teaspoon (3 ml) gum tragacanth
½ cup (120 ml) very warm water
3 tablespoons (45 ml) sandalwood
1 tablespoon (15 ml) benzoin
1 teaspoon (5 ml) powdered orrisroot
1–1½ teaspoons (5–8 ml) saltpeter

Combine the ingredients as directed on pages 22–23. Shape incense as desired and allow to dry.

An Autumn Walk

Gathering ingredients for incense can add a new dimension to walks. Stop and sniff the different plants along your way. Pick ones that are pleasingly fragrant—after you've identified the plant—and dry them for future use. We find that plucked plants are often perfectly preserved in the basket that generally gets left in the car. Try pinches of the plants on burning charcoal to decide which ones smell good when burned

On your walk, keep an eye out for these fragrant ingredients:

- Bayberry leaves
- Cedar greens
- Hemlock needles
  (the tree, not the plant)
- Juniper berries
- Monarda leaves and
  flowers
- Oak leaves

- Oak moss
- Peppermint leaves
- Rose petals
- Spruce needles
- Sweet gum tree bark
- Woodruff leaves
- White pine needles
- Yew needles

A WALK IN THE WOODS

This recipe makes us think of wonderful treks in the woods. The earthy and piney notes blend into a lovely combination.

½   teaspoon (3 ml) gum tragacanth
½   cup (120 ml) very warm water
2   tablespoons (30 ml) powdered cedar wood
1   tablespoon (15 ml) powdered sandalwood
2   teaspoons (10 ml) frankincense
1   teaspoon (5 ml) copal
1   teaspoon (5 ml) juniper berry
1   teaspoon (5 ml) powdered orrisroot
1½ teaspoons (8 ml) saltpeter
3   drops each of cypress, cedar, fir, pine, and patchouli
    essential oils

Combine the ingredients as directed on pages 22–23. Shape incense as desired and allow to dry.

CLEAR THE AIR

Use this recipe to clear the air after a house has been closed for a period of time or following a bout of sickness. The ingredients will take away the mustiness and help to disinfect the air.

½	teaspoon (3 ml) gum tragacanth
½	cup (120 ml) very warm water
2	tablespoons (30 ml) powdered cedar or pine wood
2	teaspoons (10 ml) dried eucalyptus
1½	teaspoons (8 ml) benzoin
1	teaspoon (5 ml) dried rosemary
½	teaspoon (3 ml) camphor gum
1	teaspoon (5 ml) powdered orrisroot
1	teaspoon (5 ml) saltpeter
3	drops each eucalyptus, peppermint, and lavender essential oils

Combine the ingredients as directed on pages 22–23. Shape incense as desired and allow to dry.

KITCHEN SPICE INCENSE

Here's one to remind you of kitchen smells — a somewhat exotic kitchen, but a kitchen, nonetheless.

½	teaspoon (3 ml) gum tragacanth
½	cup (120 ml) very warm water
3	tablespoons (45 ml) wild cherry wood
4	teaspoons (20 ml) benzoin
1	teaspoon (5 ml) ground coriander
1	teaspoon (5 ml) dried allspice
1	teaspoon (5 ml) dried thyme
1	teaspoon (5 ml) cardamom seed
1	teaspoon (5 ml) ground cinnamon bark
1	teaspoon (5 ml) ground cloves
1	teaspoon (5 ml) powdered orrisroot
	A few drops essential oils of your choice
2¼	teaspoons (11 ml) saltpeter

Combine the ingredients as directed on pages 22–23. Shape incense as desired and allow to dry.

VANILLA LAVENDER

Try this mellow combination, which smells of restful lavender and vanilla, if you want to relax after a hectic week.

½	teaspoon (3 ml) gum tragacanth
½	cup (120 ml) very warm water
8	teaspoons (40 ml) sandalwood
1	tablespoon (15 ml) benzoin
4	teaspoons (20 ml) dried lavender
1	teaspoon (5 ml) powdered orrisroot
20	drops lavender essential oil
1½	teaspoons (8 ml) saltpeter

Combine the ingredients as directed on pages 22–23. Shape incense as desired and allow to dry.

Six Secrets for Success

1. When making your own recipes, keep a lit piece of charcoal nearby to burn bits of plants or drops of oils. Sometimes things do not burn as well as you might think. Amber resin, for example, smells wonderful—except when it is burning. A pinch of powdered orange peel is lovely—a lot is not. So try burning pinches of items under consideration before incorporating them into a batch of incense.

2. Use a mortar and pestle, probably the ultimate mixing tool for incense. It gets everything smooth and evenly distributes the ingredients, especially the saltpeter.

3. Make small batches and keep notes. You can always make more—if you wrote down what you did.

4. On the second day of drying, knock cones over onto their sides. If they stay too close together or stay in one position, they can and will become moldy. Be sure they are in a place where there is plenty of air circulation.

5. Small cones dry faster and burn better. The temptation to make giant cones is strong. Try to resist it.

6. Use three times as much wood as resin. Otherwise, the resin will smother the wood and the incense will not burn properly.

Resources

These companies offer many of the items discussed in this booklet, as well as complete kits, quality commercial incense, and related products (such as soap or candles).

Natures Garden
Candle Supply Company
www.naturesgardencandles.com

The Rosemary House and Gardens
www.therosemaryhouse.com

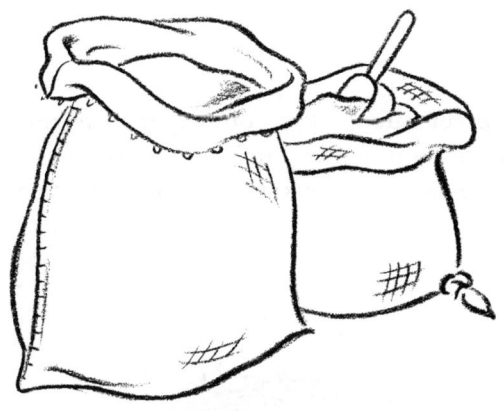

Other Storey Books You Will Enjoy

The Aromatherapy Companion by Victoria H. Edwards
The most comprehensive aromatherapy guide, filled with profiles
of essential oils and recipes for beauty, health, and well-being.

The Essential Oils Book by Colleen K. Dodt
A rich resource on the many uses of aromatherapy
and its applications in everyday life.

Hands-On Healing Remedies by Stephanie Tourles
150 recipes, using all-natural ingredients, to make your own
topical remedies to soothe everyday ailments.

The Herbal Home Spa by Greta Breedlove
A collection of easy-to-create personal care products that
rival potions found at exclusive spas and specialty shops.

Herbs for Natural Beauty by Rosemary Gladstar
Maintain a beautiful appearance with these herbal recipes
for creams, scrubs, elixirs, serums, and shampoos.

Making Aromatherapy Creams & Lotions by Donna Maria
101 recipes, using all-natural ingredients and following five easy
steps, to make your own creams, lotions, body rubs, moisturizers,
and lip balms.

Join the conversation. Share your experience with this
book, learn more about Storey Publishing's authors, and read
original essays and book excerpts at storey.com.